**NEW JOB! SLOW START?**

# TOP 10 SALES TIPS FOR COLLEGE GRADS

## JOYCE JOHNSON

www.selfpublishn30days.com

*Published by Self Publish -N- 30 Days*

**Copyright 2018 Top 10 Sales Tips For College Grads**

All rights reserved worldwide. No part of this book may be reproduced or transmitted in any form or by any means electronic or mechanical, including photocopying, recording or by any information storage and retrieval system without written permission from Joyce Johnson and Joyce Johnson Enterprises

Printed in the United States of America
ISBN: 978-1986801140

1. Sales 2. Student Success
Joyce Johnson and Joyce Johnson Enterprises.

**Disclaimer/Warning:** This book is intended for lecture and entertainment purposes only. The author or publisher does not guarantee that anyone following these steps will be a successful business leader. The author and publisher shall have neither liability responsibility to anyone with respect to any loss or damage cause, or alleged to be caused, directly or indirectly by the information contained in this book.

# TABLE OF **CONTENTS**

**Acknowledgements** ............................................................. 1

**Introduction** ........................................................................ 3

    1. First Day of Work ....................................................... 7

    2. Elevator Pitch .......................................................... 21

    3. Networking with Intent ......................................... 35

    4. How to win with the gatekeeper ....................... 47

    5. Appointment setting via email .......................... 57

    6. Effective Trial Closes ............................................. 67

    7. Overcoming objections ........................................ 77

    8. Follow up ................................................................ 89

    9. Don't Sell Alone .................................................... 99

    10. Working remote ................................................ 109

# ACKNOWLEDGMENTS

To the best editor ever Jacci Williams, welcome back! Welcome back! Welcome back! I'm not sure how I got through the first book without you. Thank you for reaching out to me the first time you noticed an error in one of my LinkedIn articles and offered to edit my work for free because you love me. You should call my sister Yolanda; she may make you an honorary sister.

Thank you to my family, friends, and mentors who have invested in my life – My Village!

My Mother, Patricia Toliver, I have often said I thank God for you because he could have put anyone in charge of me, but he gave me you. For that, I am grateful and feel extremely blessed. My siblings Ervin, Rodney, and Yolanda (Shelly), you bring me joy, support, and more love than I can hold. I hope you've felt the love I have for you. The extended siblings, the cousins I love you, and I'm proud to know such a giving, loving, smart, and passionate group of individuals. We are family and friends.

My fabulous, amazing Aunts Mabel, Elizabeth (Marie), Lillian, and Rachel. Wow, you women bring everything to the table! I want to be each of your wrapped in one when I grow up.

As the firstborn grandchild, I shared a special relationship with both my maternal and paternal grandparents. So many lessons, I hope to share someday. They along with my father, step-father, and uncles are now my angels, thank you.

I mentioned in this book to, "Build a relationship with your team members. They will become your work siblings and long-time friends." I've been blessed to meet people in the workplace selling that are still good friends; Rain Jordan, Graciela Villasenor, LeVan Moment (I traveled with him to Thailand in 2017), Quincy Harden (who makes me laugh out loud and is my financial planner), Chrystal Taylor, Michelle Bell, Tiffany Misleh, Jasmine Garrett, Tonya Anderson-Mason, my partner in crime, along with my Cousin Glenda. I appreciate learning, sharing, and growing old together.

My nieces Chalise, Erin, Kennedy, and my Godchildren Bryant, LaTara, and Leslie for you I wake up and work at being the best me. I hope this book inspires you to be great at whatever your heart desires. I love you with my whole heart. To all of the youth in my family. I expect great things, and I hope this body of work will open doors to give you a better future. I love each of you.

My publishing coach, Darren Palmer – God sent me an angel! We may have to adopt you.

# INTRODUCTION

"Top 10 Sales Tips for College Grads" is the second in a series to educate college students, their parents, and mentors on the sales profession. As graduation approaches, many students begin to feel anxiety around finding a job in their industry. My earlier publication, "Why Sales for College Students," introduced students to the sales profession, and now it is time to understand some of the basic skills and tools needed for a successful career.

Prior to starting any new job, you want to prepare for the first day of work. Most people will wait until the first day of work to begin preparing or refreshing their skills. Waiting to prepare is like limiting your study time to the one night before an exam that impacts 70% of your grade. Even if you pass, the anxiety level of the day is vastly increased. It is highly recommended that you begin preparing for work the day you decide or realize that you need a job. Day One is the first chapter of the book to assist you in jump-starting a great career.

There are 10 chapters/tips in this book, but there are many additional tips and strategies within each chapter. When you have absorbed the knowledge this book imparts, you will be fluent in basic sales terminology and well on your way to developing needed sales skills. This content will arm you with the tools to start your first day of work with confidence.

Most companies will provide in-depth training programs. However, you will want to study and understand some of the basics ahead of time. Read each chapter of this book at least twice and please, please, please take notes. Note pages are included to help emphasize the impactful skills that you will be wise to adopt.

Writing out information you obtain is a great way to retain what you have read or heard. Taking notes is essential, especially when talking with your business leaders and mentors. If someone is willing to invest their time to share the knowledge that took them years to acquire, it should be treated with the reverence and respect you would give to any person of stature whom you admire. Remember that you are tapping into a treasure trove of experience that is well worth your time and attention. Listen intently, and be diligent in your note-taking.

Continuous personal development will help you throughout your career. Continue to train, not only within the confines of the work environment, but also on your own. Read books, listen in on webinars or podcasts, and attend networking meetings or conferences. Education never ends for those who achieve great success.

This book is a guide to support you in launching your new sales career. Read, take notes, study hard, apply yourself, and be great in all your endeavors!

*Happy Selling!*

TIP 1

# FIRST DAY OF WORK

Congratulations! You landed your first job after graduation. The first day of any job is both scary and exciting. It is like the first day of your high school senior year. You are excited and filled with great expectations as you enter the building that first day; yet, apprehensive about your ability to meet course requirements, the arduous journey toward the final goal of graduation, and getting accepted into the college of your choice.

Back then, you were given summer reading assignments and a school supplies list, and then, you showed up in the new school year ready for your first-day assignments. How can you know that you are prepared for your first job? At most, an employer may request you show up with proper identification to complete the requisite paperwork for their Human Resources Department. It might inspire you to consider the adage, "How you start is how you finish." Let us start smart.

Experience tells us that taking some important time to relax before starting the new job allows for valuable time to consider what it is you want from your employer and in what capacity you wish to utilize the knowledge with which you have acquired .It is also beneficial to complete those personal tasks for which you normally need time off during the work week, get rest, get organized, and prepare mentally for your first day. It bodes well for that person who, during the interview process, remembered to do their homework looking into the background of the establishment, asking insightful questions about corporate structure, history, aims, and values.

Hopefully, you inquired about the goals and objectives expected of you in your new position, questions like: who your ideal clients are, how would you interact with them and what are the expectations and long-term goal of the position? These are key notes with which you will want to be armed, if not covered in the interview, providing you with valuable material for developing a plan.

### TOP 10 SALES TIPS FOR COLLEGE GRADS

## PREPARATION

First, understand your new employer. What do you know about the company outside of industry news? Have you sold their product or service in the past? Is this your first job? Probably not. Do you use their product or service? It is highly unlikely, however, that you will know everything there is to know about your employer, but you can have a general understanding of the offers you will represent. Dive a little deeper than you did for the interview. Seek out a fellow team member or two for a casual discussion or make a lunch date with them, and explore their perspectives. Beware of overthinking things, but definitely give some thought to familiarizing yourself with your employer and its product.

Print out the job description to which you responded during your job search and create or review the checklist you prepared for the interview. Do you fully understand the role to which you have committed? In the book "Why Sales for College Students," we discussed sales roles. How will you impact the business? Will you hunt (acquire new business for the company) or farm (sell within an existing customer base)? Are you an inside or outside representative?

Who are your customers? If you support a base of existing customers, google their businesses, set alerts and follow them on social media. If you are hunting, create a short list of companies you may want to pursue. You may want to engage a few friends or family members for help in compiling leads. It is customary for your company to have a targeted list, but if not, taking actions like these will give you a leg up on the competition. Often, smaller companies will not have a perpetually updated database, if they have one at all. In some cases, the business owners will look to you to do both, hunt and farm. Refer to the notes that you took diligently when your manager first shared the short-term goals of your working team.

You may be thinking why I should go into so much depth to equip myself for my new job? Consider the famous quote about the Lion and the Gazelle. You may have seen it in my recent publication, "Why Sales for College Students." The story goes like this:

> *Every morning in Africa a gazelle wakes up and knows it must run faster than the fastest Lion or it will be killed.*
>
> *Every morning a lion wakes up and knows it must outrun the slowest gazelle or it will starve to death.*
>
> *It doesn't matter whether you are a lion or gazelle when the sun comes up you better be running.*

## TOP 10 SALES TIPS FOR COLLEGE GRADS

Before you start running, set a goal toward where you are going, create a plan and then execute. Sounds like a lot of planning just to get started, but it will pay off in the long run. You will want to continue preparing for your new position with a 30-60-90 day plan. These are considered best practices amongst highly successful people. Plan now to build your successful future!

# THE PLAN

There are some who believe that simply setting goals is equal to creating a plan for success. A goal is just what it says, a target, a destination, that point at which you hope to arrive. Hope, however, is not a plan. A plan is how you will reach your goals within a targeted timeframe. What actions will you take to get there? It is a good recommendation to write down a plan and track the results. Again, how you start is often how you will finish. Take time to create a 30-60-90 day plan. Once you set a goal, work backward to document targeted actions. What follows is an example.

First 30 Days

1. Complete training

2. See Top 10 customers

3. Close two deals

How will you complete the above? If training has been scheduled for the second week of employment, that leaves you with two weeks to see customers. You may be thinking you have at least three weeks to see these goals through. Take a closer look.

| Week 1 | Week 2 | Weeks 3 & 4 |
|---|---|---|
| New hire paperwork | Training | Meet Top 10 |
| Training pre-work | Study, Test | Follow up |
| Initial customer email Introduction | One-hour a day customer Follow up email | Schedule appointments, close |

## 31 – 60 DAYS

The next 60 days depends on the complexity of the process, the size of the territory, and what your closing cycle necessitates. You should establish very aggressive goals to confer with as many customers as possible. Set goals, create a timeline, and plan out how you will see them. What is the best way to manage your day? One method might be, if you have a territory where customers are located within 15 to

20 minutes of each other, you can set a goal to make three visits before lunch and one after. **Activity drives Results!**

Your Schedule may look like this:

*Customer visits; 8:30, 10:00, 11:30, and 2:00*
*Follow up, proposals and next day prep 3:00-5:00*

Assuming you have checked the working hours, begin at 8 a.m., give your customer that first half hour from 8:00-8:30 to get settled, if not, they may spend time multitasking during your meeting. This can cause your meeting to run long and result in throwing off your schedule for the rest of the day. Use Monday mornings or Friday afternoons for additional training and administrative tasks. Most customers hold their internal meetings on Monday mornings. Your management will likely be doing the same.

## 61 – 90 DAYS

Repeat activities from your initial 60 days. Schedule a one on one with your manager during the last week of the month to review your progress. It's time to inspect what you expect. If your activity remained consistent, you should have achieved the results you hope for. If you have not achieved the results it's time to check and adjust the "How" of your activity. For instance are you not setting enough appointments, submitting proposals or asking for the business. Your manager and mentor should ride along with you and provide coaching. In the interim maintain your activity. Continue to make calls, schedule appointments and ask for business.

## EXECUTION

Aggressive goals and a great plan are not necessarily a guarantee of success. You need to <u>*take action and execute*</u>! Consistency is key! You must consistently see new customers and host meetings around new opportunities. This is because you will likely come across a few large, high-maintenance customers that characteristically want to meet and discuss non-revenue-generating activities.

Try scheduling them after your confirmed new-business meetings and opportunities. Follow up and Customer Service meetings are important, but take caution not to schedule ten of them in one week. Schedule 30-minute conference calls and request additional business during noncritical selling time. **Consistent, high volume activity is needed to meet your goals.**

Start your first day of work mapping your goals and making sure that they align with the expectations of the management team. Create a plan that includes a realistic, achievable amount of activity and execute consistently, week after week. This is not only the tactical part of your business but also the core of it. Once you master this area of business, you can meet with your manager or mentor to develop strategic selling goals.

Take time before reading the next chapter to write out a plan, and take time to measure and check off your accomplishments every week.

JOYCE JOHNSON

# MY PLAN

**GOALS**

_____

_____

**PREPARATION**

_____

_____

**THE PLAN**

_____

_____

**EXECUTION**

_____

_____

TOP 10 SALES TIPS FOR COLLEGE GRADS

# NOTES

JOYCE **JOHNSON**

# **NOTES**

TOP 10 SALES TIPS FOR COLLEGE GRADS

# NOTES

JOYCE JOHNSON

# NOTES

TIP 2
# ELEVATOR PITCH

So, tell me about yourself. This is a question all of us are asked throughout life in both personal and professional situations. How prepared are you for this question? What is your response likely to be? Are you likely to respond from a personal or professional standpoint or a combination of both?

Let us explore by recalling your best college pick up line. Oh, come on now, everyone has a pickup line, men and women alike. You shared your name, hometown, what you were studying, and if you played any sports or instruments. You probably modestly shared that you possessed a great sense of humor and a rich love for reading the classics. Then comes the creative close, "Would you like to go to a concert or movie this weekend?" Think about it. You have always had an elevator pitch, that point at which you close the deal with just the right question that evokes a positive response. One might ponder, just exactly how effective was that pitch, after all.

## JOYCE **JOHNSON**

The concept of an elevator pitch is to effectively communicate the five W's (who, what, when, where, and why) in the timeframe of an elevator ride, approximately 30 to 90 seconds. Some literature will quote a two-to-three-minute pitch. If you are on an elevator for that length of time, it is more than likely broken. Unless you are paralyzed in a state of panic, you will have had time to close the entire deal, with signed contracts and all. Bottom line is: be brief.

The elevator pitch is specifically devised to prepare for those unplanned opportunities. Your potential client will perhaps be transitioning from one appointment to another, or they could be entertaining a business guest or spending personal time with family and friends. Value their time and get the job done right as succinctly as possible, and if not, leave the door open for another occasion. Express gratitude for the opportunity to speak. Being sincerely respectful of their time will be rewarded when the next opportunity presents itself. They are likely to be more receptive, recalling your thoughtfulness from the previous experience.

Wikipedia defines an elevator pitch as:

> ... *a short sales pitch; that is, a summary used to quickly and simply define a process, product, service, organization, or event and its value proposition.*

## TOP 10 SALES TIPS FOR COLLEGE GRADS

Use the description that works best for you. It is not about which theory you use. The elevator pitch is about closing. This methodology is used to schedule an appointment to discuss your company's product or service. Let us assess the information needed to build a successful pitch.

<u>Who: [NAME], [TITLE], representing [CORPORATE ENTITY]</u>

Who are you? A question I asked myself recently, embarking on the journey of an author. Many of you are preparing for graduation or are recent graduates. You are not the same person who walked onto the campus that first day. At graduation, the commencement (i.e., beginning, start, onset) ceremony is designed to close out one chapter of your life. The commencement marks the transformation into one who possesses the knowledge that qualifies you for your chosen vocation. Who are you, Post College Student? I challenge you to not only define your professional self but also to cultivate your personal brand.

I was introduced to a very effective exercise in my first year of college, during one of my communication courses. The assignment was to write a personal obituary. We were asked to ponder what we would want our legacy or mark in the world to be. How do you want people to remember you? What is it that you would want to be read or said about you when you are no longer here? Social media experts recommend that you add your brand's motto (beliefs, ideas, vision) to your LinkedIn designation. I have seen sales titles leading with words like "empowering," "game changer," and "expert."

Today, you may be a novice, but now is the time to decide who you are and what you want to be in the next year, five years, and ten years from today. Write down your goals and begin to make choices in your life that represent your brand, and then, *own it!* It is your future, and it determines what will be read or said about you when you have left this life, but more importantly, while you are still here.

It is often said that people buy from people they like and/or trust. Once that link is established, it is a natural assumption that a person of integrity would only be promoting a good product. Your success is found in the statement "people they like and/or trust." Are you likable? Do people trust you? Is 'likeability' and 'trustworthiness' an indelible part of who you are? Are these qualities strongly embedded in your current brand? If you are not sure, survey friends, family, neighbors, professors – anyone within the realm of your daily life, and ask them to describe the best and worst characteristics of your personality.

If "like" and "trust" are not included in those lists, do a brutally honest examination of yourself to find out just exactly why those qualities are missing or underdeveloped, and then adjust. Like and trust are key to your success as a salesperson. Most importantly, they are essential qualities for an overall well-rounded individual.

What is your brand? Who are you?

What: Schedule a Meeting to Discuss a (Company, Product or Service)

Why: Product or Service Value/Impact to Their Bottom-Line (Value Statement)

The What and Why of your pitch are the twin sisters of Burger King. They ask for what you want to *match* what they have, and then, they tell you why they should have it your way.

## KNOW YOUR COMPANY

My work is traditionally with companies that are number one in their industry. When you can add that to your resume, it gives you an edge but not a guaranteed win over your competitors in the sales field. The high standard of the company or product you represent will go a long way to garnering favor with potential clienteles. Knowing your brand provides a unique bullet point for your elevator pitch and will figure prominently in your follow-up meeting.

The company I currently work for has a maternity-leave program which includes two weeks of paternity leave for new dads. It is a source of great pride to be a part of an organization that recognizes the importance of having a father present in the birthing process and the initial bonding stage of an infant's life. The resulting lifestyle change necessitates the father being present in the home with the recovering mother when a baby joins the family.

Without consciously planning it, the news of this great benefit worked itself into my sales presentation. It became a huge hit with my customers -- they loved it! In response, they began to share their own company policies, and the conversation often led to some personal stories about childbirth. The dialogue was rare, honest, and heartfelt, and it set the tone for a relaxed meeting environment. It was a lesson well learned that childbirth is a cheerful experience for nearly everyone, and a company's commitment to family life is well received and respected amongst potential customers.

It is good to be familiar with the bottom line aspect in

any sales presentation, but it is even better to create a universal connection that will spark conversation at any level. Companies are built by people. Learn what is important to people and their expectations of the companies where they are employed.

## KNOW YOUR CUSTOMER.

What if you recently learned through diligent research that your potential customer has a new CEO and he made a particularly revealing public statement about the team to which you are selling? Include that statement in your pitch and convey to them how your product will help to address the issues that are specific to their needs. You have now separated yourself from, and moved ahead of the competition. It may be a huge undertaking to track all of the entities that fall under your oversight, but familiarizing yourself with the top three (3) to five (5) and fully engaging with them, to the extent that it is possible, will give you an edge on the competition.

When: This Week or This Month?

The "when" of appointment setting will be discussed more extensively in a subsequent chapter of this publication. Suffice it to say that if your elevator pitch occurs prior to the 15th of the month, it is recommended that you ask for a meeting in the current month. After the 15th, request an appointment in the following month. Setting appointments should not appear as a plea of desperation, but an opportunity to discuss a benefit for both parties. Your schedule should be booked approximately two weeks in advance.

Where: Office? Over Breakfast? Or Lunch?

It is a matter of personal preference, but I like holding my first meeting at a customer's office, which is an effective tool in getting a feel for the personality and energy of the company. Try to meet all the team members or as many as you can, and set up a tour of the facility, if possible. If you established a favorable connection, anything is possible. Recently, I joined forces with a team member at a site he services. The customer had set the tone that there was not much time to spare for the meeting. He let it be known that his team was extremely busy and that no tour was available. Ultimately, we spent two hours with him, he called in his team to share their experiences, and we were eventually given a full tour of their top-secret facility.

### TOP 10 SALES TIPS FOR COLLEGE GRADS

## PRACTICE

Is it time to prepare your elevator pitch? There is no time like the present. Here is the bottom line regarding pitches; create a personal pitch about yourself to use when networking with people who can support you in the capacity of sponsor, mentor or friend, in addition to having the pitch to sell the company and product you currently represent. Let us follow the age-old motto of the Boy Scouts of America: **be prepared**!

*So, now, tell me about yourself!*

## JOYCE JOHNSON

# NOTES

**TOP 10 SALES TIPS FOR COLLEGE GRADS**

# NOTES

## NOTES

**TOP 10 SALES TIPS FOR COLLEGE GRADS**

# NOTES

TIP 3

# NETWORKING WITH INTENT

Dale Carnegie said, in his world-renowned book "How to Win Friends and Influence People," "You can make more friends in two months by becoming interested in other people than you can in two years by trying to get other people interested in you."

Once, having been told that I had mastered the art of networking, I pondered the validity of the statement and whether I had actually attained that lofty goal. It became apparent to me that to truly master the authentic art of networking, you must apply yourself diligently to developing the best techniques for consistently connecting with your target buyer. When networking, I intend to make a connection with someone who can become a friend, mentor, sponsor, someone I can help or someone who can help me. It may be someone who is already in my sphere of daily life. It will likely be someone who shares my interests and commitment to family and community.

JOYCE **JOHNSON**

As business professionals, we all receive our share of invites to weekly business networking events. We sign in, grab a name tag and add our business card to the evening's raffle. Networking, the act of meeting new people in a business or social context, as defined by Wiktionary, became a business buzz word over a decade ago. The question is, how effective are you at networking? Networking has helped me to form relationships lasting 20 years, both personally and professionally.

## **MAKE A CONNECTION**

Take a moment to think about the last event you attended. Did you make a connection with anyone? If you call their office, will they immediately take your call? If you invite them to an event, will they accept? Drum roll, please: will they refer a business associate to you or accept a referral from you?

To make a connection, one must sincerely take an interest in the person(s) you meet. A connection is made when two or more individuals find a commonality that joins them together. While networking, it is essential that we focus less on personal agendas and instead commit our full attention to the conversation.

## TOP 10 SALES TIPS FOR COLLEGE GRADS

To establish a good connection, you must take note of three important aspects of the people you meet:

1. *Company and industry*

2. *Business goals*

3. *Personal history and interests*

Most people you meet will be equipped with their own elevator pitch, thereby providing you with quick answers to Notes One and Two. Note Three, however, may take a little time and effort on your part. This is where the rubber meets the road. This is where you make the connection. Carefully navigating this particular area provides valuable insight and will help you tap into a personal vision. It can lead to the realization of dreams, inspiring unique business concepts and promoting new business ventures. The value of Note Three cannot be stressed enough. It goes a long way toward developing strong personal and business relationships that can last a lifetime.

An opportunity to network was given to me some years ago with a gentleman in the hotel industry. As we shared our mutual information, it came to light that he was CEO of the family business. Later, a friend shared with me his plan to develop property he owned in the Bahamas. He mentioned he was looking for a hotel partner. Recalling the connection that I had made with the hotel entrepreneur, it seemed an obvious choice to facilitate a connection between these two potential partners.

Now, here is where cultivating Note Three to the fullest extent pays off. Because of our positively-charged meeting, a busy hotel CEO recognized and opened my email. We made a connection that may develop into a major business partnership. Hence the Art of Networking!

So, get out there and meet as many people as possible, exchange cards or numbers, but remember to take time to make that valuable connection, first and foremost. Be of the mindset that asks, how can you support this person or what they do? How can you partner up to invest in others? Do your networking with the intention of connecting with people on a personal basis, as well as professional. Develop a resource pool from which you can glean amazing partnerships which can lead you to become an agent for change in today's market of disruptive collaborations.

**TIME TO GIVE BACK**

Do you remember how this chapter opened, with a famous Dale Carnegie quote? "You can make more friends in two months by becoming interested in other people than you can in two years by trying to get other people interested in you." In the previous chapter, did your personal elevator pitch volunteer efforts? When you wrote your obituary, did it include a commitment to public service? It is a true tenet of human nature that when you give freely, you will receive abundantly. Taking the time to listen and take mental notes is key to the Art of Networking.

One of the best places to connect with a future customer is at a benefit event or a fundraiser. A parable from the Book of Luke in the Bible states, "To whom much is given much is expected." The most successful people are the ones who give back to their family members and friends, to the needy, to the community, and generally, to making the world a better place. You will find most business owners or leaders you meet have a cause about which they are passionate. Whether or not you share an interest in the same organization, the commitment to volunteer work and giving back will promote a united connection when that next opportunity for networking is presented.

The mother of a good friend relocated to a new environment having retired from her career. Instead of enjoying the free time, she found herself bored and wanting to get back to work. Enduring interview after interview, there had not been a single offer. She signed up for volunteer work during an election period to keep herself busy. She showed up every day to her post on time and gave it her best. One day, during a conversation with another volunteer, she shared her career path, transition to retirement and the experience of moving. The person with whom she was talking was a manager who by chance had a position open. It was a job for which this retiree was perfectly qualified. The interview was set, and she began working within weeks. Volunteering was not a calculated effort to find employment, but it led to an opportunity for intentional networking among volunteers, and the desired job found her. Get out and volunteer, and then, get to know the people around you.

## SOCIAL MEDIA NETWORKING

It is said that Facebook connects you to people you used to know, LinkedIn connects to people you know, and Twitter connects you to people you would like to know. An old theory, citing, "Six degrees of separation," could probably rank second or third in today's environment of social media. A social media platform offers an opportunity to connect with a person or company of interest. Be wary of connecting to anyone with whom you are not prepared to respond or meet.

## TOP 10 SALES TIPS FOR COLLEGE GRADS

Social media has probably launched more careers and initiated more connections than any other platform. Social media is the best way to learn information about potential customers, recruiters, and business leaders with whom you will interview for your first or next job. On the upside, social media can be your connection to new and exciting life; or on the downside, it can have you blocked forever.

When reaching out through social media, ensure that your posts professionally represent your brand. If the content does not represent your current brand, it is recommended you cancel that page and start a new one. With that said, keep in mind most things on the World Wide Web cannot be completely erased. If someone shared your comments on their pages, you can only delete your own post, not theirs, the likes, retweets or reaction history. Remember that what you share will be forever attainable in cyberspace by future employers and business partners. So, network wisely and safely with intention, and be thoroughly prepared and informed.

So, all you Masters in the Art of Networking, go be intentional and network!

JOYCE JOHNSON

# NOTES

# NOTES

JOYCE JOHNSON

# NOTES

## NOTES

TIP 4

# HOW TO WIN WITH THE GATEKEEPER

Like most sales people, you will try almost anything to get past that one person with a cold, stern face or tone that reads, "Don't even think about it!" It is the much-regaled and largely maligned Gatekeeper. The Gatekeeper manages the telephone calls and messages, often holds down front desk duties, maintains the appointment schedule, and in some cases, oversees the boss' email. If you offend the Gatekeeper, it will be like watching paint dry before you ever get past him or her to secure a future meeting. If you find yourself in trouble with the Gatekeeper, be automatic with a humble smile and a sincere apology. If you are uncertain as to whether or not you have offended the Gatekeeper, you can always verify.

Then follow up with your most sincere apology. Everything you need to know about winning with the

Gatekeeper you already learned by the age of ten (10). Your parents and elders taught you three basic courtesy skills that are useful in all aspects of life. We learn early on how to win friends and influence people by employing three simple tools of courtesy: greeting, complimenting, and inviting.

Whenever possible, greet the Gatekeeper by name. If you do not know it, ask for it, and write it down. You will want to add this crucial information to the contact lists in your electronic devices and in the customer relationship management (CRM) system. On the fly, you can text or email this information to yourself, along with any other facts you learn about them or their family. Even the most militaristic Gatekeeper can be charmed by someone who cares enough to recall the little tidbits of their lives gleaned from a previous encounter.

On sales appointments in the field, I have had several opportunities to observe the interactions of salespeople with their Gatekeepers. The technique is often reflected in the resulting follow-up opportunities. Here is a case in point. For the past year, an account manager consistently complained about not getting an appointment with a key stakeholder. With a little intervention on my part, a meeting was finally confirmed. Once we arrived, I noted that he treated the Gatekeeper like she was a robot that speaks. The only communication was his name, the company he represented, and who he wanted to see. I approached the counter with my hand extended, offering up a smile and a warm hello. We discussed the weather and my lack of preparation for traveling to the east coast during winter. As we were escorted to our meeting, the Gatekeeper and I exchanged wishes for a great day to one another.

Following the meeting, as we exited the building an hour later, our Gatekeeper called out to me, "Safe travels, Joyce." A pleasant and personalized greeting is a good icebreaker and goes a long way toward engaging that all-important front desk person. Always greet your Gatekeeper!

You have a daily ritual: the suit, shoes, hair, makeup, a little something extra that makes you smell good, all that goes into making your best impression. You want to look and smell your best every day, and you hope it is not overlooked. You want to walk into the office and have a flood of compliments that make your head tilt upward a little higher. What works for you, also works for the Gatekeeper.

Follow up your greeting with a nice, sincere, good old-fashioned compliment. Who doesn't enjoy a good compliment? Consider the Gatekeeper's day and how the morning unfolded. They started out early, kids, spouse, carpool, traffic, and the deer that darted out in front of them just before turning into the parking lot at work. As soon as things calm down, in walks the "charming" salesperson without an appointment. What sets the mood is that our charming salesperson is equipped now with a warm greeting and a genuine compliment. Take time to greet and compliment the Gatekeeper.

Greeting and complimenting your Gatekeeper creates a rapport that will lead to a solid working relationship. There is a sweet payoff when you take the time to learn a little more about their likes and dislikes, friends and family, and then you seal the deal by sharing information of an upcoming event which may be of interest to the Gatekeeper. Extending an invitation can go a long way. Yes, even the dreaded Gatekeeper deserves to enjoy a nice outing and an opportunity to treat the family.

Often, it is the Gatekeeper who receives and disseminates the information when an invitation is given to the team members in the office for a company function. Although unintentional, excluding the Gatekeeper can come across as discourteous. Even if the Gatekeeper is not able to attend, he or she will appreciate and remember the gesture. You just made the

## TOP 10 SALES TIPS FOR COLLEGE GRADS

Gatekeeper's day with a pleasant greeting, a flattering compliment, and a personal invitation to include them in your plans.

Our parents taught us these basic manners at an early age because they know that greeting, complimenting, and inviting (being inclusive of others) are critical keys to our success. Carry these actions in your proverbial box of tools and practice them until they are a natural part of your personal brand.

Remember, the Gatekeeper has a job to do. If you make their day easier, the Gatekeeper will help you *win!*

JOYCE **JOHNSON**

# **NOTES**

# NOTES

JOYCE JOHNSON

# NOTES

TOP 10 SALES TIPS FOR COLLEGE GRADS

# NOTES

TIP 5

# APPOINTMENT SETTING VIA EMAIL

*I hope this note finds you smiling!*

What were your first thoughts after reading the above statement? Have you ever received an email greeting from someone wishing you a smile? Think about your favorite greeting from an email or text. Maybe it was "Hello, Beautiful," or "Good morning, My Love." When I call my brother, Rodney, he answers, "Hello, my Beautiful Sister" and it always makes me smile. An endearing greeting attracts the reader and sets the tone for a productive engagement. The truth is, I can be found calling my brother during a challenging day to hear that special greeting for a midday pick-me-up. It is likely unsuitable to greet your customer as "beautiful," but you can certainly draw from your creative spirit an applicable term of endearment.

Setting appointments by email is not as simple of a task as it seems. There are three easy rules to follow when it comes to making a favorable contact by email and obtaining that coveted face-to-face meeting. Before we get into that, let me recapitulate our opening sentiment: *I hope this chapter finds you smiling.*

## RULE #1
## BE CREATIVE IN YOUR GREETING

"I hope this note finds you smiling!" The first time someone receives this greeting, there is nearly an immediate response of, "Thank you! Now that I have been reminded, yes, I am smiling." This greeting is, as we say in Texas, "mighty hospitable." It takes the receiver off-guard, activates the smile factor, and boosts neurotransmitters like dopamine. You have just activated some of the best stress relievers known to medicine. Keep in mind that not only is your subsequent client likely to be "wearing multiple hats," but the businesses of today are running at an absurdly fast pace. Anything you can bring to the table that helps to value, comfort, and brighten the day of its recipient is likely to work in your favor.

On a project where the contact was notoriously less than prompt in responding to emails and telephone messages, an ostensibly errant follow-up message invoked an immediate response. The email read, "I hope this not finds you smiling!" The amused contact responded with, "Why don't you want me to smile?" The takeaway is this: whether or not this incident was an oversight or a shrewd attention-getter, it worked, did it not? Be creative in your delivery. You might also want to be diligent in your proofreading.

## RULE #2
## KISS - KEEP IT SIMPLE, SWEETHEART

From a time management perspective, you will have approximately one or two hours at the start or end of your day in which to make calls for new business, and to follow up on existing opportunities. You will need to make the best of your time. The same is true for the people you will be contacting. Their time is also limited and should be valued. Keep your messages brief. Avoid prolonged explanations. Your first, and preferably only paragraph should reflect the who, what, where, when, and why of your communication. Research has shown that the average hurried businessperson retains only the first few lines of an email; so, capture all that you can in one paragraph.

Ask yourself honestly if you like getting lengthy emails from customers or vendors. After getting lost in the maze of excessive verbiage, you find yourself having to decide whether or not to invest even more valuable time in a telephone discussion for clarification. If paring down the content is not an option, try using bullet points for a more concise explanation of the highlighted issues. Let us think for a moment on that obsequious school paper, where we were instructed to incorporate an opening statement, three supporting bullet points, and then, the closing. Funny, is it not, that all this time, you thought high school English would never pay off.

## RULE #3
## ASK FOR THE APPOINTMENT

As previously recommended, securing a firm commitment for an appointment has its emphasis in offering a definite date and time (i.e., "Are you available Tuesday at 10 am or Wednesday at 2 pm?") This method most often works in your favor. If not, you might try asking your contact if they have a couple of preferences for a meeting within the next two weeks. This approach works for most; however, consider your target audience. It may not be realistic to obtain a meeting with the CEO of a major national company or government official within the desired two-week timeframe. When requesting time with high profile individuals, it is recommended that you widen the margin to the next four weeks and send two date-and-time slots that work best for you.

## TOP 10 SALES TIPS FOR COLLEGE GRADS

This third approach affords your key contact a more plausible availability, and at the same time, you have relieved them of the obligation to provide their own scheduling options, which would likely result in the consumption of more time. Offering two date-and-time preferences also benefits you by reducing the likelihood of calendaring errors.

Rule numbers 1, 2, and 3. In Rule #1, we see that the greeting allows you to build an effective rapport. Rule #2 reminds us to keep it simple, be brief and respectful of time. Rule #3 helps to enrich our appointment outcome with varying approaches to establishing a meeting time and date. These strategies have been tried and true. My 20 plus years in sales has taught me that more appointments directly equal more closed deals. Then, follow up, follow up, follow up. If the expected result still eludes you, remember "The Second Agreement – Don't Take Anything Personally," from the bestselling book, *The Four Agreements* by Don Miguel Ruiz.

*I hope this note has you smiling!*

## NOTES

TOP 10 SALES TIPS FOR COLLEGE GRADS

# NOTES

JOYCE **JOHNSON**

# **NOTES**

**TOP 10 SALES TIPS FOR COLLEGE GRADS**

# NOTES

TIP 6

# EFFECTIVE TRIAL CLOSES

A Trial Close is not a <u>normal</u> **"closing technique"** but a test to determine whether the person is ready to **close**. <u>This method is good for use after a presentation or after you have made a strong selling point. Use it also when you have answered objections.</u>

The above statement is only a half-truth. Trial closing is a technique to determine if the customer is ready to close but it is so much more. Trial closes should be used from the beginning to the end of a deal. A trial close will help you understand the customer's "Why," as well as their budget and any existing urgency to move forward with a purchase. Getting a "yes" is good but understanding why you are getting the "yes" is **great!**

Always Be Closing ("ABC")! This is such an old saying in the world of sales; yet true. Have you ever had a sales rep run past you with a proposal in hand, headed to see a customer? You exchange pleasant remarks, and their "happy" demeanor seems to shout, "I am about to close this deal!" Many salespeople misinterpret the proposal and/or presentation meeting as a guarantee of the close.

Historically, it may have been an accepted norm to assume that a solid sale would result from a positive conversation. Today's customers are way too savvy to allow themselves to be "trapped" by such assumptions and will utilize tools like your corporate website and other data on the World Wide Web (www) to carve you out of their decision-making process. The psychology for this is to have the customer sell to you! You will find this methodology in the following sections. After incorporating these gems into your sales style, wait – simply wait – and then just wait until you see the results!

## TOP 10 SALES TIPS FOR COLLEGE GRADS

Listening is key, which is why it is being reiterated here, in addition to being strongly advised in other chapters. There can never be enough stress in this particular practice. Take notes and highlight what is important to your potential client. Spending too much time expounding, without allowing valuable feedback, devalues the prospective customer and depletes the established rapport. Think of this process as a conversation with someone whose opinion and knowledge requires your respect, like a long-standing mentor or a grandparent. (Grandparent? Yes! Was it not a significant part of our historic American culture for many years, that when a grandparent speaks, we are called to rapt attention and respectful listening?)

Remember that this is a conversation in which there is an exchange of words, concepts, and expressions. Relax and enjoy the ride. Your prospective customer is an individual with unique qualities and perspectives. Explore and use them to promote a positive outcome. Replace the standard question-and-answer meeting with the approach of having a cup of coffee with a good friend.

When scheduling the appointment, articulate a desire for getting to know the person with whom you are meeting and what it is that they represent. Express your sincere interest in exploring their needs. This goes a long way in providing a comfortable environment; however, let us not get too comfortable. As a presenter, you must stay alert and on your toes.

## TRIAL CLOSE – STEP #1

Understand why a program, service or product like the one you are promoting important to your customers business. The customer knows the answer. He/she or they have likely researched your product or service and possess at least a surface understanding of the benefits. If your meeting request was accepted, they have already figured out that your product may suit their needs. In your encounter, listen carefully, repeat responses for clarification, take notes and ask appropriate follow-up questions. It is important that you capture the essential "Why" that motivates the customer's needs. Your attention to such detail is the muscle behind clenching the deal.

## TRIAL CLOSE – STEP #2

Understand how your product increases revenue or lower costs for your customer. The financial impact may not be clear to the potential client. Referring back to Step Number One, now is the time to determine what your prospective customer plans to accomplish; then walk them through it, providing answers with each step. Do not give it all away too soon. Some information increases in value, as the plan unfolds and your potential client begins to understand the benefits.

You may have to ask follow up questions to uncover when and/or how your plan can be utilized for maximum impact. Will the product or service save time, space or money for the business you are servicing? Will it increase production or provide improved service to the internal or external clientele? Will it simplify a current process?

Once you have received answers and fully qualified the why, the next question might logically be, "Is there an approved budget for the program?" Upon determining the financial parameters, your natural instinct is to jump headlong into the cost discussion. Resist the temptation to do so. This information possesses a far more favorable reception as interest in your product/service is cultivated.

## TRIAL CLOSE – STEP #3

You may open this phase of your presentation with, "What is your strategy for implementing this system?" Allow time for a response and spend time exploring the options. Walk them through the best practices of other models that mirror the business to which you are customizing your presentation. Write it out on a presentation board or a sheet of paper, providing a visual enhancement to the discussion. A standard implementation may only take only one page, but it is worth the time and effort to draw out a plan. Having it all on paper benefits both the customer and you as a point of reference to be employed during the recommended recap of your meeting.

Something to keep in mind is that everyone wants to know and feel that their project is unique. Maintain eye contact and show sincere interest in the business concerns of the person with whom you are meeting.

Many sellers will tend to skip this step (i.e., implementation plan). It is not necessarily what I advise. Step Number Three promotes yet another level of commitment, which may or may not be an effective tool for your desired close. It might proceed as follows:

> *Great Mr. or Ms. New Business! Since you have decided to purchase my product/service, shall we get started on completing our agreement?*
>
> *Will you be my point of contact, or will someone else own the project from this point going forward?*
>
> *Here is how I recommend we proceed . . . .*

Happy Closing!

TOP 10 SALES TIPS FOR COLLEGE GRADS

# NOTES

# JOYCE JOHNSON

# **NOTES**

**TOP 10 SALES TIPS FOR COLLEGE GRADS**

# NOTES

JOYCE **JOHNSON**

# **NOTES**

TIP 7
# OVERCOMING OBJECTIONS

*"Every sale has five basic obstacles no need, no money, no hurry, no desire, no trust."*
**– Zig Ziglar**

Overcoming objections can be easier if you effectively use your trial closes, as previously laid out in the prior section of this publication. The decisions made by business owners and decision-makers begin with a perceived notion that your product or service is nonessential; they may have a fear of income loss; perhaps it is the concept that there is plenty of time to make such a change; or it could simply be a complete lack of interest. It becomes your task to determine which of these barriers to a successful sale exist and why.

The bottom line here is that if there is no need, no money, no hurry, and no desire, all of your work to build a trustworthy relationship with your potential client may still be ineffective, but building trust helps to lay the groundwork for what must follow. Building a strong foundation of trust may not conquer the five basic obstacles, but you may find yourself getting that golden referral that results in a major sale or a valuable relationship.

## IDENTIFYING THE NEED

Remember that first trial close? Why is a program, service or product like the one you are promoting important to your target business? It must be determined early on whether your potential customer truly has a need for your product, or if they are only fishing.

Why would they be fishing? There are many reasons for this, they may have been introduced to a similar program by one of your competitors and they are exploring their options. This does not necessarily indicate an impossible sale, just that you will have to work harder and longer at revealing the "why" and convincing them that your product is better.

Addressing the customer that has an answer to that question can be tricky. Although they understand their "why" and that a need exists, you will want to consider that there may be something else holding them back like money or trust. They may trust you implicitly, but they may not trust that the product or service you represent will perform up to their expectations. This is a valid fear.

Unless you are dealing with a major risk-taker, most businesses fear loss of income, and with it, the possibility that it could escalate into a forced business reorganization. Such fear could outweigh any need an organization has. They may be thinking they can patch up what they currently have rather than risk potential debt. This is where you, the educated expert, keep them talking about the true need for your product or service and the positive impact it will have on their business.

If the competition is selling the same or similar product or service, you will need to concentrate on selling the "why" by building trust, thereby encouraging them to partner with you and your company.

Educate your potential customer on the benefits of working with you, your company and your product. Share industry insights and recognizable awards and standards set by your company. Then engage them in the learning process by testing what they know. Share the wisdom that makes your listener the educated expert! They will appreciate you for the experience and for equipping them to sell the project internally. When the representative of your potential customer is excited to share the benefits of your company, product or service with the management and colleagues of their own establishment, then you know you have nailed it!

## UNDERSTANDING OBJECTIONS

It is customary for there to be a list of popular objections compiled over the history of the company whose product and/or service you are marketing. It is advantageous to become intimately familiar with these objections. You may have some of your own to add to the list. Study the objections diligently and be ready to use them where needed in your initial conversation with the perspective customer.

Understanding potential objections empowers you to ask better questions and provide better answers in the process of educating your customer on your product. The better prepared you are to identify and address concerns during the initial conversation, the greater the opportunity to deliver a closing presentation.

Listening is Key! After all, were we not gifted with two ears and only one mouth?

Remember that first day when you left training in your new job? You were pumped, energetic and confident that you were armed with more information than the law could possibly allow, ready to run out the door, equipped with your objections list, and ultimately destined to convince the very first person with whom you meet that they were going to love and purchase your perfectly-pitched product! Hold on there, Slugger! Slow down! If you have not mastered the art of listening, all the training in the world will not serve you well.

Listen! Listen, *and* take notes. (If note-taking is via digital device, it is important to convey this to your potential customer.)

Once again, there is a reason we have one mouth and two ears. Listening is a significant technique because what is important for you to hear is not always in the words that are said, but in the message behind them. Even if you are well-prepared with your objections list, the customer may not always be direct in their communication. You may have to listen intently to hear between the lines. What do you hope to learn by listening? What is it that is really behind the obstacles of no need, no money, no hurry, no desire, and/or no trust?

- *No need* – investigate and resolve, if possible; walk away, if necessary,

- *No money* – short-term vision can seem insurmountable, explore long-term budget options

- *No hurry* – make sure your answers match the needs of the moment; as necessary, move communication to once a month, add to six month forecast

- *No desire* – if there is no resolution after a mutually respectful exchange, it might be time to walk away

- *No trust* – prepare to walk away, but share your company's social media sources, as the burden now lies in business marketing

**DO OVER? OBJECT TO THE OBJECTION!**

Recently, it was noted that a site procured by one of my internal clients was not buying from the new contract. It was a mystery, as he generally does a great job selling the value of the partnership. We scheduled a meeting with the local account manager to go on-site for a tour and to have a conversation with the key stakeholders. The plant manager was "tied up" and unavailable for the initial introductions. By design, we moved the group into the plant area where we would be more likely to meet up with the plant manager.

**TOP 10 SALES TIPS FOR COLLEGE GRADS**

Before the question was asked why he had not been engaging our team for support, he blurted out, "I know I should be buying from you guys and that your company provides good service, but I have worked with my favorite rep from XYZ Company for many years. He is awesome and provides me with great service. When he changed companies, I changed with him to his new business." Then the chatter amongst the ladies was that he is a very nice-looking man. One of them said, "I think he might be single, too," laughing out loud! Seems this guy had plenty going for him.

Not willing to accept the situation, and compelled to think quickly on my toes, I countered with, "If we hire him to work at our company, then will you buy from us?" His response was enthusiastically affirmative. "Great," I said, "give me his name and number and we will get our recruiting team right on it!"

In a seemingly lost cause, find a way to win! Think on your toes. Learn what makes the other guy so great AND **be that good!**

JOYCE JOHNSON

# NOTES

## NOTES

JOYCE JOHNSON

# NOTES

## NOTES

TIP 8

# FOLLOW UP

*"Get up, Show up, Follow up!"*
— **Joyce Johnson**

According to, 'Youtech & Associates' study on the importance of following up, 80% of sales are made after five or more follow-up calls. However, only 10% of sales professionals follow up after their fourth contact. You may be thinking following up seems simple, and it is, but even the best salespeople find themselves discouraged and ultimately settling for the low-hanging fruit.

Consistent follow up opens doors to success and supports previous efforts toward building trust, cultivating personal and product value, and promoting sales opportunities.

JOYCE **JOHNSON**

## BE CONSISTENT

Follow up consistently. The practice of sales is centered on statistics. There is a lot of data in sales, and all of it points toward the fact that consistency leads to success. During initial training as a new hire, your company may have shared its winning matrix of leads that have proven historically successful in the industry. There may also be a list of required activity-minimum parameters. For example:

[A] amount of calls will result in
[B] amount of scheduled appointments

[C] amount of appointments will result in
[D] amount sales opportunities

[W] amount of sales opportunities will result in [X] proposals

[Y] amount of proposals will result in
[Z] of closed deals

The above activity drives consistency. If your activity is consistent, your sales will be consistent. Why? Your activity gives you more opportunity for increasing your business potential. Consistency demonstrates to your employer a propensity for augmented sales with increased revenue.

### TOP 10 SALES TIPS FOR COLLEGE GRADS

## BUILDING TRUST

If you recall, trust is a consistent theme throughout several chapters of this book. Trust is important in all relationships, and the best salespeople understand that their most important task is managing relationships. Managing national relationships on behalf of my company for a particular vertical market has proven to me from early on that the stronger the foundation of building relationships, the better the sales.

Your product or service may cost more, take longer to process or be the alternative brand of choice, but if you have a good relationship with the customer and they trust you, a lucrative and lasting business transaction can be yours.

The manager of a previous employer called to discuss a customer with whom he was concerned because sales were down and the customer was not communicating. He wanted my insight on how to turn things around. I weighed in only after hearing from him that the new sales representative had been in contact only by telephone, versus getting out and meeting his clients face-to-face.

Being a huge advocate of personal engagement, I advised that meeting in person is an essential part of building trust with a potential customer. Personally,

I will brave the rain, the sleet, possibly even the snow to build a significant rapport for closing the deal.

You may be confident in all the groundwork you have laid out to procure the business of a potential customer, but if you find yourself in a major disagreement, then, first and foremost, as abhorrent as it may seem, ***the customer is always right*** (even when they are not), and second, do not for one second think that you can solve the issue over the telephone. You really need all of the facets that a face-to-face meeting can give you in order to make headway.

## PROVIDE VALUE

In sales, we often use the words "rapport," "relationships," and "partnerships." These are industry buzz words used to create a portrait of value. They are used to convince the customer that we have his or her back and will go above and beyond what is required to earn their trust and increase their business potential. Take the time, however, to totally grasp what is important to the decision maker, their leadership, and the team. It may not require a material action on your part, but a logistical one. They may be interested in a training seminar, or they may be in need of a product not sold by you. When you read an article that may prove helpful or meet someone who can add "value" to the business of your potential customer, share this information with them. Add value to your potential representation by being a resource for your customers, even though it may lead to a portion of money flow going to a business other than your own.

## FOLLOW UP

Get up, show up, and follow up consistently. When creating your action plan, remember that success comes from showing up. When planning territory visits, communicate what day and timeframe you will be in the area, and if you have to move a proverbial mountain to do it, be as true to your word as is humanly possible. If your schedule calls for being out of the office, keep your strategic contacts informed. Always set your out of office email and telephone announcements with an allowable specificity. Your clients will grow to depend on you to deliver. Because you have established reliability, they will wait until Wednesday for something they needed Monday, simply because they know you will show up. Follow up consistently, build trust, add value, and grow your business.

JOYCE **JOHNSON**

# **NOTES**

# NOTES

JOYCE JOHNSON

# NOTES

TOP 10 SALES TIPS FOR COLLEGE GRADS

# NOTES

TIP 9

# DON'T SELL ALONE

*"If you want to go fast, Go alone.
If you want to go far, go together."*
**– African Proverb**

To sell alone is bad. To lose alone is tragic. Today, companies have so many resources available to sellers: mentors, managers, product specialists, agents, trainers, and sales effectiveness teams.

Do you remember being a kid and wanting to go to the park or bike riding? Did you go alone or call on your friends on the block to accompany you? More than likely you called a friend or two to follow along. Why? You would have 10 times the fun with your buddies than you would by yourself. The same applies to sales. There is a team of people you can take along for the ride to help develop your skill set, help you close, and will be committed to your success.

JOYCE **JOHNSON**

## WORK ASSIGNED MENTOR

On your First day at work, you will be assigned a mentor. This person will be a team member or someone in your department. Mentors are sometimes paid a percentage of your initial compensation; others may volunteer to fulfill their personal development plans, or they just pulled the shortest straw. Either way, your assigned mentor's role is to get you started by showing you around, introducing you to other team members and staff, maybe getting you set up with work materials and answering those initial questions.

Keep in mind this person may become a friend of yours, but they are not, yet. Save the complaints for home. Even if your mentor is frustrated and begins to complain, do not get pulled into the negativity. Remain neutral and remove yourself from the situation. Watch your language; you are no longer in the dorm. Your mentor is assigned to provide a sense of comfort to your transition of starting a new job.

## TEAM MEMBERS

Build a relationship with your team members. They will become your work siblings and long-time friends. They will help you research internal products or services or competitive information, finish that proposal that is keeping you at work late, and connect you with the right people to support your success. You want to invite team members individually for coffee or tea and conversation. Like with your customers, listen for something that connects you to your peers. Say thank you often and take advantage of opportunities to return a favor or offer support.

*Help them first.* Your team members will have sales experiences to share with you, but remember, you have a database of skills also that could help them when creating presentations or proposals. I love working with college students because your information is new or updated. College students have exposed me to using apps to pre-schedule social media posts, shortcuts, and updated features to Excel and PowerPoint, and how to incorporate video. Treat team members like your customers, add value, be a resource. Be a team player.

## LEADERSHIP

Your biggest cheerleader, motivator, teacher, and resource is the person who hired you. She or he has bet on you and is vested in your success. With that said, they have other team members to support as well and expect you to utilize your resources and figure some things out on your own. You must be smart and resourceful. Your leader will give you information and direction. Your manager will also set your goals and communicate expectations of the job. If you do not fully understand expectations, ask questions.

Meeting goals and expectations is why you were hired. Gain clarity on your responsibilities and execute. Engage your manager to attend customer appointments. They will guide you and share best practices.

Again, you will have opportunities during one-on-ones and ride-alongs to learn from your leaders, but you are one of many they support. You will need to obtain the information, then pull from your own bag of tricks to make it happen.

## TEAM ADMIN

Your number one resource! Know this person's name, children or grandchildren, favorite snack, hobby, and sports team. The admin is clearly the best salesperson on the team. He or she has networked through the company, listened in on leadership conference calls, scheduled meetings, traveled for senior leadership, and knows everything about everyone of influence. The admin is the orchestra director and will connect you to resources it could take you years to learn. Be respectful and helpful to your new best friend.

## TOP 10 SALES TIPS FOR COLLEGE GRADS

### INTERNAL RESOURCES

Identify your internal sales resources and take them to every meeting until you are comfortable going alone, and even then, include them. They know the company and product, and in most cases, their pay is tied to the sales numbers. Your teammates may join you on a call, but they have their own goals to meet, and your leader's time is shared. So, these guys are in place as experts to help add credibility and support to close business.

### YOU ARE YOUR BEST RESOURCE.

Believe in and use your instincts to guide you through good and difficult situations. Know which conversations to have internally versus externally. Remember that your parents, uncles, and aunts have worked for years and may be able to guide you through corporate politics.

You bring to the table the newly developed tools via technology. Continue to invest in your education by joining professional organizations. Attend educational networking functions and annual conferences. Your company may have an annual budget to support membership fees and attendance. I am guessing the team admin will know or direct you to the right person.

***Don't Sell Alone.*** You are surrounded by resources of people who are committed to your success. Stay connected to the ***Why Sales For College Students*** family on social media and email me through LinkedIn. I look forward to hearing about your journey to becoming a ***top seller!***

TOP 10 SALES TIPS FOR COLLEGE GRADS

# NOTES

JOYCE **JOHNSON**

# NOTES

TOP 10 SALES TIPS FOR COLLEGE GRADS

# NOTES

JOYCE **JOHNSON**

# NOTES

TIP 10

# WORKING REMOTELY

Many companies are moving away from brick and mortar office spaces and tending toward working remotely. The story was told in my first book, "Why Sales for College Students," of my first sales experience after college with a Dallas company for which I marketed alarm systems offsite. In all honesty, I would not recommend a remote position for your first job.

On the other hand, if the opportunity for growth and success exists, and if the company provides extensive product and sales training, along with access to local resources to support you, then, by all means, go for it. Seriously consider the levels of support at your disposal and prepare for any eventuality by asking the questions that promote clarity regarding the internal support you hope to receive. Working remotely sounds great; however, it has its pros and cons. Let's talk about it!

JOYCE **JOHNSON**

## PROS OF WORKING FROM HOME

When the topic of my working from home arises, the first reaction is nearly always, "Wow, I would love to have that kind of freedom!" Trust me, if the job is to be done properly, there are but a few freedoms.

1. True, you do have the freedom to bypass the snares of working in the office environment and instead establish a more direct and expeditious route to your customers. There are so many distractions in the office that can cost you valuable time in keeping appointments. Living in Houston, a very busy industrial area rich with traffic congestion, I find that leaving early provides a much needed jumpstart to the commute. The chances of doing this from a busy office fraught with its multiple demands and unscheduled complications are slim and none. Another advantage is that, when your meeting runs late, you will not have to deal with the stress of getting back to the office for that inevitable end-of-day check-in meeting with your manager.

2. Probably the most popular reason for working from home is that you can stay in your pajamas throughout your administrative duties. For video conferencing, just throw on a jacket, comb the

hair, and add the finishing touches (ladies add their lipstick), all the while remembering the imperative: do not stand up.

3. Flexibility is another desirable aspect of working from home, but it can go both ways, pro and con. Working remotely allows you the opportunity to manage your own schedule, a feature afforded many sales jobs. In my experience, the creative juices seem to flow best after unwinding from meetings, calls and emails, often leading to late working hours and ultimately a delay in the next morning's schedule. The clock, as I write this chapter, registers 1:11 a.m. After concluding my work day at 6:00 p.m., watching, "This is Us," and sending follow up emails until 11:00 p.m., I was finally ready to create.

## CONS OF WORKING FROM HOME

1. **Flexibility** – This can actually be a deficit to freedom! This chapter has had snapshots of my typical day, starting with a 7:30 a.m. telephone call. Working from home has its demands. There are days you will miss breakfast and lunch. Because you work from home, co-workers who may have access to your calendar could assume that a 15-minute break means they can schedule you into a telephone conference.

2. **Perception** – An inexperienced manager, or one who micro-manages, may view any open space on your calendar as an opportunity to infringe on your schedule. The general perception is often skewed toward the fallacy that working remotely constitutes a laid back, non-eventful daily work environment. Not true. Interruptions are an undeniable part of any workday, but even more so when you work from home. Documenting every telephone call and each task as they occur throughout the day is essential to effectiveness and efficiency. So, document, document, document!

3. **Time-management** – This, too, is both a pro and a con. Much like the description of my day when penning this chapter, you may find yourself continuously working late into the evening hours and not shutting down. Social engagements may often take a back seat to work. Here is where we come dangerously close to becoming a workaholic. You can thwart this by setting guidelines and timelines and sticking to them. This applies even to scheduling of downtime for rest and to attend social events. Proper time-management produces the quality of life for which we all yearn.

## TOP 10 SALES TIPS FOR COLLEGE GRADS

Here is a final note concerning the writing of this chapter. This content replaces a previously-planned chapter on sales and revenue forecasting. This topic will be covered in my YouTube video blog. The need for this information was brought to my attention after connecting with several recruiters seeking entry-level sales professionals to work remotely. So, you see, there is a niche for you if working remotely is what you hope to attain.

Larger organizations can offer the support and resources you need to be successful. So, use them. Create a general work habit or daily schedule and follow it. Do not neglect to Include your workout, breakfast, and time with family and friends.

**NOW GO AND SELL SOMETHING!**

JOYCE **JOHNSON**

# **NOTES**

**TOP 10 SALES TIPS FOR COLLEGE GRADS**

# NOTES

JOYCE JOHNSON

# NOTES

TOP 10 SALES TIPS FOR COLLEGE GRADS

# NOTES

www.ingramcontent.com/pod-product-compliance
Lightning Source LLC
Chambersburg PA
CBHW070148230526
45471CB00002B/572